3/77

ROYAL BRITAIN IN COLOUR

Royal Britain
in colour

Introduction and commentaries by
Garry Hogg

B. T. BATSFORD LTD
London

Acknowledgments

The Publishers would like to thank the following for permission to use photographs:
British Tourist Authority for pages 47, 49, 51, 53, 55 and 57
Camera Press for pages 31, 33, 59 and 61
Central Office of Information for page 33
Central Press for pages 23, 39 and 43
Fox Photos for pages 17, 19, 21, 25, 27, 29, 37, 41, 45 and 63

First published 1976
© B. T. Batsford, 1976
Text filmset by Servis Filmsetting Ltd, Manchester
Printed and bound in Hong Kong by
Leefung-Asco Printers Ltd,
for the publishers B. T. Batsford Ltd,
4, Fitzhardinge Street, London W1H 0AH

ISBN 0 7134 3108 3

Contents

Introduction

Of the round score of monarchies that survive in the world today, the oldest by many centuries is that of Japan. Though following his country's defeat in World War Two, Hirohito renounced his claim to divinity, he does claim to be descended from the Storm God Susanoo and the Sun Goddess Amaterasu; since he is the 128th descendant in a direct line, that claim takes the lineage back beyond history and into the realm of mythology, and so may perhaps be discounted, save by traditionalists.

Historians find it less easy to establish the oldest monarchic line surviving in Europe to this day. Norway's claim is strong, for it was back in the ninth century A.D. that the near-legendary 'Harald-the-Fair-Haired' swore not to shave off his beard until he had united the internecine states of that country. Scandinavia as a whole being in a state of turmoil, he had taken on an almighty task. Sweden to the east and Denmark to the south were permanent threats; overlordship ranged from one country to the other, and as a matter of strange fact, Harald's Norway did not achieve complete independence until the early years of the present century.

Denmark has, marginally, a stronger claim. Danish historians claim that their small country's first monarch was one 'Gorm the Old' (a less attractive sobriquet than Harald's), who ruled in the first half of the tenth century; Queen Margrethe of Denmark claims direct descent from him, in effect establishing a 1,000-year lineage. But, like Norway and Sweden, her country has over the centuries been involved in complex inter-relationships of rule, surrendering to superior strength here, recovering status there, sharing authority with others; today, she is a monarch, but she does not wear the crown; the last coronation in Denmark was a long century ago.

What, then, of Britain, the only other contender in these stakes? Our early history, following the departure of the Romans in the fourth century, to some extent resembles that of Scandinavia: small kingships and kingdoms, the rise and fall of dynasties-in-miniature resulting from the fluctuating powers of the various tribes that crossed the North Sea and settled here, dividing the territory on which they landed for periods of varying lengths. Some established themselves more quickly, and more lastingly, than others; Jutes, Angles and Saxons, from Denmark and Germany, consolidated their positions during the seventh century. Kent became the 'kingdom' of the first-named; Saxons established the kingdom of East-Saxony – Essex. Angles established the larger kingdom of East Anglia. Others spread northwards into today's Midlands – their Mercia – which extended from Offa's Dyke, on the Welsh Border, to the North Sea coastline. Others again spread even farther north, to establish the kingdom of Northumbria. Perhaps the strongest Saxon contingent moved westwards, the South Saxons giving their name to Sussex and the West Saxons to Wessex, which was to become the most powerful of all these regional 'kingdoms'.

During these exploratory, consolidating, years, between the seventh and the mid-tenth centuries, no fewer than sixty self-appointed kings rose to power, ruled for long or short periods, were deposed, or died in battle against rival kings or, more rarely, of old age. But these were still regional kingdoms only. It was not, in fact, until the early years of the eleventh century that one of them put out his claim to be 'King of all England'. The son of King Sweyn of Denmark, Canute (or, strictly, Cnut), came to England at the age of eighteen; two years later, on the death of his father, he became king of England and, like his father before him, of Norway and Sweden too. At the age of thirty-two he led his army north across the Scottish Border and defeated King Malcolm; he thus became the first true King of Britain, and remained so until his death in 1035 A.D. His great kingdom then fell apart. He himself was buried at Winchester – appropriately enough since the city had been the heart of the Kingdom of Wessex, largest of all the regional kingdoms.

Better known to history than Cnut, and certainly a more remarkable man, a ruler, law-maker, traveller and scholar, was King Alfred, youngest son of Ethelwulf, one-time King of Wessex, whose life had filled the second half of the previous century (he almost certainly died in 900 A.D.). Though he was continuously at war against the Danes, he never claimed to be king of all England, though his son, self-styled 'The Unconquered', Edward the Elder, made the claim for himself as early as 924 A.D. His claim was demonstrably false, for he never succeeded in conquering the Danish Kingdom of York, and his own kingdom ranged no farther north than the Humber.

These remote chops-and-changes of monarchic supremacy may seem irrelevant, or over-emphasised, but they are outlined in order to point the distinction between the uncertainty of those distant centuries and the relative stability of those that were to follow. Cnut was truly king of all England when he died in 1035 A.D., and the country was to be united again under Edward, styled 'The Confessor', seven years later; but he left the ruling of his kingdom first to Earl Godwin and then to the latter's son, Harold, while he devoted himself to an essentially religious life and the rebuilding of Westminster Abbey, where he was buried in 1066. It was in January of that fateful year that Harold was elected king, as the record puts it, 'by popular acclaim'; he reigned for nine months before meeting defeat and death at the hands of William of Normandy's army during the Battle of Hastings.

In spite of the various claims to overall sovereignty, most historians accept that William the Conqueror was the first true King of England. Being the man he was, he well merited his title; but though ruthless to his enemies, he reigned for some twenty years until his death in 1087, and governed both wisely and well. He had the foresight to establish what is known as the Salisbury Oath; this obliged all the lesser landowners who, prior to his coming, had had to swear fealty to their immediate overlords, the powerful barons, to swear allegiance in future direct to him, as their monarch. It was on account of that Salisbury Oath, as one recent historian put it, that 'England became for ever a kingdom, one and indivisible'.

During the near-nine hundred years between the death of William of Normandy and the ascent to the throne of our present queen, some forty monarchs, kings or queens, have reigned over this country, though the sequence was temporarily interrupted in the seventeenth century by the Protectorate of Richard and Oliver Cromwell that lasted for a mere decade. 'The continuity of the monarchy,' the official record declares, 'has been broken only once in over 1,000 years; in spite of interruptions in the direct line of succession, the hereditary principle on which it was founded has never been abandoned.'

The statement appears to contradict the one made in an earlier paragraph. But it is justified by pointing out that the lineage of Queen Elizabeth II can be traced back not merely to the eleventh century, when Malcolm II ruled over Scotland, but before him to Alpin, King of Kintyre, and before him to Egbert, for twelve years King of England in the early ninth century. It is this fact that makes this country's monarchy a strong rival to that of Denmark. Purists have argued that genealogists have permitted their imaginations to run riot over these remote claims in attempting to produce documentary evidence; perhaps it is *lèse majesté* to challenge their findings.

Nor, really, does it matter all that much. Suffice it that this country has been a monarchy for many, many centuries and – for the foreseeable future at any rate (in spite of the subversive activities of a rebel few both in and out of Parliament) – is likely to remain so; those who are opposed to the principle of the monarchy may be growing in number, but they remain an undistinguished minority.

It is interesting to note the extraordinarily close ties that still exist within the small group of royal families in Europe, echoing, as it were, the far-distant times when kings of Norway, Denmark and England reigned for long or short periods over one, two or even all three at once. Inter-marriage here has a long tradition. Christian IX of Denmark, who occupied that throne during the second half of last century, earned the not-inappropriate title, 'Father-in-law of Europe'; four of his offspring occupied European thrones – in Denmark, Russia, Greece and England; his daughter, Queen Alexandra, was married to our own Edward VII. Our present queen is related to Queen Margrethe of Denmark through no fewer than seventeen generations, and is married to Prince Philip, great-great-grandson of Queen Victoria and grandson of King George I of Greece; and his mother was Queen Elizabeth's mother's cousin.

There are close royal links, too, with Norway, whose present King Olav, son of King Haakon, had for his mother the daughter of Edward VII and Queen Alexander. As an odd footnote to this network of inter-marriage, King Olav was born in the royal residence of Sandringham, which Edward VII, while still Prince of Wales during Victoria's reign, did so much to develop and extend on this huge Norfolk estate.

It may all seem a little too 'in-bred' for the taste of the majority of us, however strong our respect for tradition; but as more and more of the 'Royals' decide to 'do their own thing' and marry, not members of other royal houses but commoners of their own choosing, the web must inevitably, and almost certainly for the better, be broken. There are already signs of this: though Olav of Norway married Princess Martha of Sweden, in the old tradition, their three children have all married commoners. Crown Prince Harald married Sonja Haraldson (the name has remained a popular one ever since the ninth-century 'Harald-the-Fair-Haired'), daughter of an Oslo businessman; the two princesses followed suit, each marrying a plain 'Mister'. Will Prince Charles, heir to Queen Elizabeth's throne, be the first in our land to break tradition and marry a commoner? The answer to that question may well soon be known.

★ ★ ★

The monarchy having been well and truly established by William the Conqueror and consolidated by his immediate Norman successors, there then followed a dynasty of fourteen Plantagenets, then six Tudors, then six Stuarts (interrupted by the Protectorate, or Commonwealth), then six Hanoverians; then came Edward VII, of the House of Saxe-Coburg, and finally the House of Windsor, of whom Queen Elizabeth II is the fourth member. In order to illustrate the concept of 'royalty' as it has inevitably changed down the years, it is worth glancing briefly at a representative handful of those who have occupied the throne; in a nutshell, it could be said that the emphasis has shifted from 'ruling' to 'reigning'.

The rôles played by successive monarchs have varied greatly. Henry II, for example, the first of the Plantagenets, ruled for thirty-five years, until he died in 1189; but he paid at least as much attention to his kingdom of Northern France as to this country. He was a great builder of castles: the famous

'Round Tower' at Windsor was his handiwork; so too was the equally famous rectangular keep at Dover, whose walls, twenty feet thick, rise almost a hundred feet above the inner bailey.

His son, Richard Coeur-de-Lion, was a great traveller, but essentially in the guise of a soldier at the head of a crusading army; though technically on the throne for a decade, in fact he spent barely a year in this country, occupying much of that time raising funds for his war against the Saracens. Edward I was another inveterate castle builder: three that he built in the Principality of Wales, which he coveted and conquered, are noble monuments to his ambition and imagination – Conway, Harlech and, most famous of all, Caernarvon, where Queen Elizabeth II proclaimed Charles Prince of Wales.

More has been written, and is popularly known, about Henry VIII, second in the line of Tudor monarchs, than perhaps about any other monarch until recent years: his addiction to successive wives, and disposal of them, for example; his creation of England's first true navy and, the other side of the coin, his dissolution of all the monastic houses. He, too, was a great builder of castles, as those at Walmer, Sandown and Deal, in Kent, and St Mawes and Pendennis, facing one another across the Fal estuary in Cornwall, remind us: the coastal 'signatures' of this remarkable monarch.

Elizabeth Tudor stands in a class by herself, dominating the gloriously rich age of exploration, learning and literature, as represented by such men as Raleigh and Drake, Spenser, Marlowe and Shakespeare. With the Stuarts, Charles II, William and Mary and Queen Anne came the revival of the theatre (condemned during the Commonwealth) and the emphasis shifted to elegance and the cultivation of the arts, not least in the field of architecture. These monarchs no longer built castles, let alone went to war; the very notion would have been unthinkable. Nor, of course, did the Hanoverians who succeeded them: the four successive Georges, William IV, and Victoria (the Queen would *not* have been amused!). By now, it may be said, true power had ebbed from the monarchy as such; rule was by parliament, while the monarch reigned.

As for contact between monarch and people down the years, this was virtually non-existent save for the privileged few such as the landed gentry, owners of great houses, who were the not-always-wholly-delighted hosts when monarchs set out on their protracted 'Royal Progresses' with their enormous retinues, all of whom had to be accommodated, however economically disastrous these royal visits might prove to be. The peasant working in the field may have caught a glimpse of the Progress and the townsfolk may have had an occasional opportunity to raise a cheer; but Shakespeare's memorable line, 'There's a divinity doth hedge a king', stated an axiom that there has existed since the ancient priest-king concept a barrier between monarch and commoner that could not be surmounted.

It is hardly exaggerating to say that not until 1932, when King George V first broadcast a Christmas Message to his people, including those of the Commonwealth, was any real, nationwide contact made between monarch and subject. One sentence in that broadcast epitomised the new approach: 'I am speaking to the children above all,' he said in his grave voice; 'remember, children, the King is speaking to you.' This truly human note had never before been heard down the long centuries of monarchic rule and reign; it has been sustained for the past forty-odd years, and emphasised latterly by the fact that the monarch could be seen as well as heard while speaking.

In a sense this reflects the fundamental difference between the *ancien régime* and the new, though the change may have been so gradual as to be virtually imperceptible. For centuries, the monarchs were the absolute source of executive power. During Queen Victoria's reign the political economist Walter Bagehot declared: 'By using the Royal Prerogative the monarch could disband the army, sell off all ships of war, make every citizen, male or female, a peer and every parish a university, dismiss all civil servants and pardon all offenders.' Such acts, of course, would be not merely irresponsible but suicidal, leading to inevitable civil war; even long before last century they would have been unthinkable. For a very long time past, though such all-embracing powers were possessed by the reigning monarch, they could be controlled by Secretaries of State and other high-ranking members of the government of the time.

This has long been recognised by both monarch and government alike. The Crown, historians and others stress, has enormous *theoretical* power but, in practice, little *actual* power. It remains 'the fountain of honour', able to confer peerages, knighthoods, baronetcies and various distinctions such as the V.C., the O.M., the O.B.E. and innumerable others; but it confers these on the advice of the Prime Minister or, in rare instances, some other high governmental authority. The Crown exercises an incalculable influence throughout the kingdom and the Commonwealth; but, again quoting Walter Bagehot: 'In most cases the greatest wisdom of a constitutional monarch would show itself in well-considered inaction.' Less than a hundred years later, Sir Winston Churchill observed: 'On the whole, it is wise in human affairs, and in the government of men, to separate pomp from power.' The two declarations may be read as one.

Whatever republicans may feel (and their numbers are steadily growing), the majority of us still feel that the Crown is essential to our way, not so much of life but of government; this is because it presents the continuity of the state of authority: governments rise and fall, but the Crown remains the permanent *stable* element in our constitution, superior to all controversy in the political field.

It is illuminating to study the evolution of this process down the years. From a relatively brief period when the early monarchs possessed absolute power, maintained by ruthless extermination of would-be challengers to their dominance, succeeding monarchs have more and more sought counsel with those who, they believed (though not always rightly), could advise them in the actions they proposed to take. During the era of the feudal lords there was established what was first known as the Great Council. This consisted of the monarch's 'tenants-in-chief'. They could be summoned to the Court, which in the twelfth century was held at Westminster, to advise – though their advice would not necessarily be taken; the Great Council in due time became the House of Lords, whose hereditary members still have the nominal prerogative of counselling the monarch.

In time it became evident that there must be a permanent group of reliable advisers readily available to the monarch; thus was established the Continual Council, a term which in due course came to be known as the Privy (or private) Council. In its earlier stages it invariably included the Lord Chancellor, the Lord Treasurer, and a number of bishops and senior judges; in this form it survived well into the sixteenth century, and it survives to this day, though its function has to some extent changed, and its composition too. Originally it was an administrative body; today it serves as a channel for the formal ratification and issue of the sovereign's commands, such as the dissolution and summoning of parliament or the calling up of men for the armed services in a period of emergency. From the Privy Council there are issued what are still termed 'Orders in Council', which carry the force of law. Its membership – since members remain so for life – at present numbers something like three hundred. All cabinet ministers are, *de facto*, Privy Councillors; the Speaker of the House is a member, as are the archbishops and a few eminent judges. There may be Privy Councillors who lie outside these categories, appointed as a mark of honour. Every member of the Privy Council takes – as the very term implies – a solemn vow of secrecy.

Thus the link between reigning and ruling, the distinction which Churchill said must exist between pomp and power. We now accept that the monarch reigns, while the making of laws and other essential duties are carried out by the members of parliament whom we ourselves elect. They are ordinary men and women like ourselves, though their place of work is within the walls of what is still known as the Palace of Westminster. On certain occasions, the ordinary people stand in the presence of the monarch – as, for instance, at the Ceremonial State Opening of Parliament; it is on such occasions that all that is conveyed by that simple word, pomp, is to be seen: the monarch is among the rulers.

For all that George V was the first to address his peoples by way of the microphone, he was still, by tradition, remote from them; we might be his 'children', but he was a 'father' only very rarely seen. It would be truer to say that the monarch did not really come among his people until the horrors of the blitz of the Second World War brought George VI and his Queen out into the streets of London to talk to those whose homes had been destroyed. Monarch and subject at last had something palpably in common, for Buckingham Palace, like any East London two-up-two-down, had been hit. There was no 'pomp' in this encounter, of course; just a heartening gesture of sympathy and understanding. That gesture has been echoed, as it were, very recently when Queen Elizabeth and Prince Philip left their palace and met victims of I.R.A. bombings and the police who had handled the situation and the bomb-disposal men and others involved. It is certainly true that, greatly as the commoners in the bitter war years appreciated the royal gestures, at heart, and subconsciously, in all probability they preferred that their monarch should be at a greater remove from themselves. What the current generation of victims feel is less easy to ascertain, for the whole climate of opinion as regards royalty today is gradually changing.

Even if there is not direct contact between monarch and public generally, there are many functions in which royalty may be seen going about its business *in public*. Foreign potentates are greeted at airports or on railway station platforms; the Queen may launch some newly-commissioned naval vessel; she may appear in the Royal Box at some theatre for a world première, attend the first performance of an opera or ballet or even a music hall – as at a Royal Command Performance. There is the age-old ceremony of the Distribution of the Royal Maundy; there is the laying of the wreath on Remembrance Day at the Cenotaph; there is the annual Trooping of the Colour; there is the drive-in-state at Royal Ascot; there is the royal presence at the Highland Games at Braemar.

Other members of the Royal Family are of course to be seen during many official and also unofficial functions: Princess Anne competing in Horse Trials and in Show Jumping at many venues such as Badminton and Earl's Court; Prince Philip playing polo at Cowdray Park and elsewhere, and sailing at Cowes and visiting exhibitions and unveiling memorials. There are no restrictions on sightseers crowding the road as the Royals arrive at Crathay church when in residence at Balmoral, and an audience numbering scores of thousands witness the presentation at Wembley after the annual Cup Final. A few fortunate thousands are invitees at the Royal Garden Parties held in the grounds of Buckingham Palace; a few hundreds may be present when the Royal Family, complete with corgis, step off the train at King's Cross on their return from holiday at Balmoral. And, within the last year or two, there has been a tendency – much welcomed by all save for the die-hards – for the Monarch and Prince Consort to 'go walkabout', whether in Sydney, Australia, or in London, England. These latest manifestations of a change in attitude, welcome as they are to most of us, do not of course come into the category of Royal Occasions, which for the most part are illustrated and described in the pages that follow.

THE GARTER CEREMONY

The Companionship of the Order of the Garter, founded in 1348 by Edward III, is strictly limited to the Monarch, the Royal Family, twenty-five Knights, the Military Knights of Windsor, and a handful of overseas members of distinction; its chapel is St George's, Windsor. The Investiture of a new Knight takes place in the Throne Room, an impressive occasion.

Wearing the Sovereign's Mantle of the Most Noble Order, the monarch buckles the coveted Garter on the recipient's left leg, then places the mantle and collar on his shoulders and presents him with the Star of the Order and the broad Ribbon, which is worn transversely across the chest. The newly created Knight then takes the Solemn Oath. Following this, the Kings-of-Arms, Pursuivants, Heralds and Military Knights proceed between two ranks of dismounted Household Cavalrymen to the Chapel of St George for the Garter Service. The twelve Military Knights, permanently resident in Windsor Castle, wear brilliantly variegated uniforms of scarlet tailcoats, broad-striped blue trousers, cocked hats with red and white plumes. The motto of this famous Order is, of course, the memorable *Honi Soit Qui Mal Y Pense.*

Cérémonie de la Jarretière

L'Ordre de la Jarretière fondé en 1348 par le Roi Edouard III se limite très strictement au monarque, à la famille royale, aux vingt-cinq chevaliers, aux Chevaliers Militaires de Windsor et à une poignée de membres étrangers de marque. La devise de cet Ordre célèbre est bien sûr le fameux: *Honi Soit Qui Mal Y Pense.*

Das Verleihungszeremoniell des Hosenbandordens

Der nur aus Mitgliedern des Königshauses und einigen wenigen Rittern bestehende Hosenbandorden wurde 1348 von Edward III gegründet und besitzt eine eigene Kapelle im Schloss Windsor. Die Verleihung des Hosenbandes durch den Monarchen ist ein farbenprächtiges, feierliches Ereignis.

THE QUEEN MOTHER RECEIVES A DOCTORATE OF MUSIC

Degree Day at the Royal College of Music, founded in 1883, is always a special occasion, and never more so than when, on 5th December, 1973, H.M. The Queen presented Queen Elizabeth the Queen Mother with an Honorary Doctorate of Music. The Queen is Patron of the Royal College, and the Queen Mother is both a Patron and the President. It is traditional that Her Majesty visits the College once every year, and this was a particularly memorable occasion for all.

While Her Majesty presents the illuminated Scroll to her mother, who is wearing a gown of gold and a bright blue hood and black velvet cap trimmed with gold, the then Director of the College, Sir Keith Falkner, in a red robe and silver-white hood, stands behind the royal recipient. Watching the ceremony on the platform, and facing the large audience of students, are the President of the Student Body, Roger Chase, and the Chairman of the Council, Colonel Gordon Palmer. Others present are members of the College of Music Council, Professors of Music, and certain privileged members of the Royal Household. Following the presentation of Degrees, a performance of Menotti's *Amahl and the Night Visitors* was given by R.C.M. Opera School.

La Reine Mère reçoit le titre de docteur en musique
Au Royal College of Music, fondé en 1883, le 5 décembre 1973, le jour de la remise des diplômes et devant tous les dignitaires du Collège, la Reine Elizabeth remet à la Reine Mère le titre de Docteur Honoris Causa de musique.

Die Königinmutter erhält ein Ehrendoktorat der Musik
Seit der Gründung des Royal College of Music war der Examenstag immer ein besonderer Anlass. Ganz besonders 1973, als Königin Elizabeth anlässlich ihres jährlichen Besuches in einer feierlichen Zeremonie der Königinmutter ein Ehrendoktorat der Musik verlieh. Beide sind Mitglieder des Colleges, die Königinmutter ist sogar Präsidentin.

A STATE BANQUET AT GUILDHALL, LONDON

Many banquets are held at London's Guildhall, at which the Mayor, Sheriff and Aldermen will be present according to the importance of the occasion. If it is a State Banquet being given in honour of some visiting Head of State, then Royalty will be present too. The monarch will also attend banquets given under other auspices, when diplomatically or otherwise requested. The banquet shown here was organised on behalf of the Trades Union Congress Centenary, in 1968.

The setting for these banquets, as may be seen, is magnificent, for London's Guildhall is one of Sir Christopher Wren's masterpieces. The initial reception is usually held in the Guildhall Library, from which the guests proceed to the Great Hall, on the oak-panelled walls of which are to be seen the Arms of England and other insignia and the scrolls recording the succession of no fewer than six hundred Lord Mayors of London who have held office since its inception. Officers in their traditional liveries here offer a dash of colour to what is on the whole – in view of the identities of the majority of the guests – a dark-suited body of individuals. Her Majesty, addressing the Congress, stands out from the rest in pale blue.

Un Banquet d'Etat à l'Hôtel de Ville de Londres
C'est dans le cadre magnifique d'un des chefs-d'oeuvre de Sir Christopher Wren qu'ont lieu ces banquets auxquels assistent, selon l'importance de l'occasion, le Maire, le Shériff et les Magistrats, parfois même le monarque. Les Hôtes se retrouvent tout d'abord dans la bibliothèque d'où ils se rendent à la Grande Salle aux boiseries de chêne.

Ein Staatsbankett in der Londoner Guildhall
In der Guildhall, Londons Rathaus, werden im Beisein des Oberbürgermeisters, des Kreisrates und der Stadträte Staatsbankette gegeben, an denen teilweise auch der Hochadel teilnimmt. Hier sehen wir ein Bankett aus Anlass des hundertjährigen Bestehens des Gewerkschaftsbundes, bei dem die in Hellblau gekleidete Königin eine Rede hält.

THE ROYAL MAUNDY

For some six centuries the reigning monarch has distributed this 'dole' every year on the day preceding Good Friday. The ceremony takes place alternately at Westminster Abbey (as here) or at some other prominent cathedral. In his capacity as Lord High Almoner, the Archbishop of Canterbury attends the monarch and the procession makes its way between two ranks of the Yeomen of the Guard, complete with halberds. The monarch and Archbishop carry sweet-smelling nosegays – a reminder that in less hygienic days the nobility and lawyers and others obliged to meet 'the common people' took this precaution against the risk of contagious disease.

White and red purses containing specially minted coins tallying with the age of the monarch are distributed among a number of deserving poor also tallying with the monarch's age, though today the content of the purses has been standardised to the sum of £5 apiece. Since these specially minted silver coins, small as they are, are unique, they are much sought after by collectors, who are always prepared to pay a recipient well over the true value of a piece because of its rarity. It is, however, very rarely that a recipient will part with the coins.

Aumône Royale
Ici dans l'Abbaye de Westminster, l'Archevêque de Canterbury assiste le monarque lors de la distribution de l'Aumône Royale du Jeudi Saint. Les pièces d'argent distribuées et frappées pour l'occasion sont très recherchées des collectionneurs prêts à les racheter à un prix beaucoup plus élevé que leur valeur réelle à cause de leur rareté.

Das königliche Almosen
Seit rund 600 Jahren verteilt der jeweilige Monarch jeden Gründonnerstag ein aus Sondermünzen bestehendes 'Almosen' an ausgewählte Bedürftige. Das Zeremoniell findet abwechselnd in der Westminster-Abtei (wie hier) oder einer anderen bedeutenden Kathedrale statt. Der Nasenschutz, den der Monarch und der Erzbischof von Canterbury tragen, erinnert an weniger hygienische Tage, als die Leute der Oberschicht sich so gegen ansteckende Krankheiten schützen wollten, wenn sie sich unters 'gemeine Volk' begeben mussten.

THE INVESTITURE OF THE PRINCE OF WALES

Edward Plantagenet (later Edward II) was presented by his father, Edward I, to the people of Wales in 1284; he used the words 'Eich Dyn', which strictly mean 'This is your man'. In July, 1969, Charles was presented to the people of Wales by his mother, H.M. The Queen. The motto of the successive Princes of Wales has always been 'Ich Dien' – 'I Serve'. The ceremony shown here took place at Caernarvon Castle, amid pageantry rarely seen in the Principality.

Attending were the Queen's Bodyguards of Yeomen and Gentlemen-at-Arms, members of the Sovereign's Household Cavalry, Pursuivants-of-Arms and Heralds, watching over the Royal Family, Diplomats and Peers, the Secretary of State for Wales, the Arch Druid and other notabilities. The Queen bestowed upon her son the Sword of Office, the Gold Rod, the Gold Ring, and the Crown. In the picture, his hands clasped between hers, he is speaking his solemn oath, declaring: 'I, Charles, Prince of Wales, do become your liege man of life and limb and of earthly worship.' The occasion was enhanced by the playing of music specially composed by the Master of the Queen's Musick and also by that Penillion Singing so essentially in the Welsh tradition.

L'investiture du Prince de Galles

C'est en juillet 1969 que Charles fut présenté par sa mère, Sa Majesté la Reine, au peuple gallois. La cérémonie a lieu ici au château de Caernarvon. La Reine remet à son fils l'Epée du Prince de Galles, le Bâton en or, l'Anneau en or et la Couronne. Sur la photo, le Prince de Galles, les mains dans celles de sa mère, prête serment.

Die Investitur des Prinzen von Wales

Im Jahre 1284 wurde Edward Plantagenet (der spätere Edward II) von seinem Vater, Edward II, dem Volk von Wales vorgesetzt. Im Juli 1969 wurde Charles von seiner Mutter als Prinz von Wales eigesetzt. Die abgebildete Zeremonie fand mit viel Prunk auf Schloss Caernarvon statt. Auf dem Bild spricht Prinz Charles gerade den feierlichen Eid.

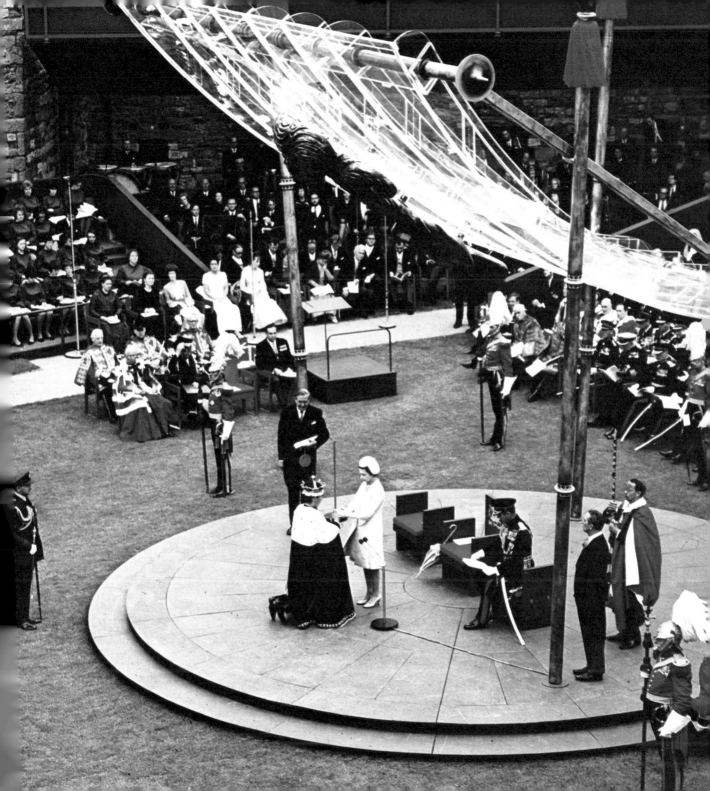

THE ROYAL COMPANY OF ARCHERS

When the monarch is in residence at the Palace of Holyroodhouse, Edinburgh, this body of men, to whom H.M. The Queen is here presenting new Colours, acts as Ceremonial Guard. Their uniform may be less picturesque than that of, say, the Yeomen of the Guard in London, but they have every right to be proud of it. It consists of dark green tunic with black facings, dark green trousers with crimson stripes, balmoral bonnet ornamented with the Company's badge and a Scottish eagle's feather. They carry, of course, the traditional long-bow and arrows.

The Royal Company of Archers derives from a body of men appointed by James I of Scotland early in the fifteenth century to develop the practice of archery throughout the land; it was formally constituted exactly three centuries ago; in 1822, King George IV dubbed the Company The King's Bodyguard and presented its Captain-General with the famous Gold Stick as seal of office. The archers have competed for the Musselburgh Silver Arrow every year since 1603; but the most important trophy is The Queen's Prize, shot for annually over an 180-yard range. By tradition, the monarch in person presents the coveted award to each year's winner.

La Compagnie Royale des Archers

La Royal Company of Archers a été officiellement constituée il y a trois siècles. Depuis 1603 les Archers participent chaque année au concours de la Flèche d'Argent de Musselburgh. Le trophé le plus important demeure toutefois le Prix de la Reine où selon la tradition le monarque en personne remet la récompense convoitée au gagnant de l'année. Cette compagnie agit comme garde d'honneur lorsque le monarque réside au Palais de Holyroodhouse à Edimbourg.

Die königliche Bogenschützengesellschaft

Die königliche Bogenschützengesellschaft rührt von einer Gruppe von Männern her, die James I von Schottland im 15. Jahrhundert einsetzte, um das Bogenschiessen im Land zu verbreiten. Vor genau drei Jahrhunderten wurden sie formell eingesetzt. Heute dienen diese Männer bei feierlichen Anlässen auf dem königlichen Sitz bei Edinburgh dem Monarchen als Wache. Seit 1603 bewerben sie sich um den Silbernen Pfeil von Musselburgh und kämpfen jährlich um den Preis der Königin.

THE QUEEN AT THE TOWER OF LONDON

In the north-west corner of the outer walls, between the Devereux Tower and the Waterloo Barracks, is the Chapel Royal of St Peter ad Vincula; here on occasion the Queen attends Evensong. Escorted by the Governor of the Tower, she passes between two ranks of the Yeomen Warders, who, though they wear the same Tudor dress as the Yeomen of the Guard, are known commonly as The Beefeaters. They are based permanently at the Tower of London.

To the south of the Chapel Royal of St Peter ad Vincula (ominous name!) a plate set in the ground marks the site of the scaffold on which Anne Boleyn, Catherine Howard, Lady Jane Grey, the Earl of Essex and countless other notabilities were executed; ironically, the site is known as Tower Green. Their remains lie buried beneath and within the chapel's altar rails, and in the crypt beneath are the remains of Sir Thomas More, and others whose memorials are on the walls. Macaulay wrote of this: 'There is no sadder spot than this little cemetery; death is here associated, not as in Westminster Abbey with genius and virtue, but with all the miseries of fallen greatness and blighted fame.'

La Reine à la Tour de Londres

La Reine assiste parfois à l'office du soir dans la Chapelle Royale de St Peter ad Vincula. Escortée par le Gouverneur de la Tour elle passe entre deux rangs de gardes dénommés les Beefeaters. Au sud de cette chapelle royale une plaque marque l'endroit où furent exécutés Anne Boleyn, Catherine Howard, Lady Jane Grey, le Comte d'Essex et tant d'autres notables.

Die Königin im Tower of London

In der Nordwestecke der äusseren Mauern liegt zwischen dem Devereux-Turm und den Waterloo Barracks die königliche Kapelle St Peter ad Vincula, wo die Königin gelegentlich an der Abendmesse teilnimmt. Südlich der Kapelle markiert eine Gedenksteinplatte den Platz des Schaffotts, auf dem zahllose berühmte Personen hingerichtet wurden. Ihre Gebeine liegen darunter begraben, und in der Gruft unter der Kapelle ruhen die sterblichen Reste von Thomas Morus und anderen.

ROYAL ASCOT

This famous Race Meeting is so called because Ascot Racecourse is located on royal land. It is fitting, therefore, that Royalty should, by long tradition, attend; it has done so for three centuries, though it was Queen Anne who made it a regular feature and inaugurated Her Majesty's Plate, with a 100-guinea prize. The first race of the meeting, to this day, is known as the Queen Anne Stakes – though the winner stands to gain substantially more than one hundred guineas! First held in August, Royal Ascot now takes place annually in June. The most important event is the Ascot Gold Cup, first offered by King George III in 1807.

It was actually the Prince Regent who inaugurated the royal carriage procession that precedes each day's racing. The royal party leave neighbouring Windsor by car, but change into open carriages in what remains of Windsor Forest. The carriages are drawn by the famous 'Windsor Greys', complete with mounted escort of outriders. Thereafter, the members of the Royal Family take their places in the centre of the grandstand, flanked by those fortunate enough to have found seating there. Formal attire prevails, since the monarch and citizens are virtually rubbing shoulders.

Royal Ascot
C'est sa situation sur territoire royal qui a valu à cette course son qualificatif. En effet, par tradition la Royauté se devait donc d'y assister. Le Prince Régent inaugura le cortège royal en carrosse qui précède la rencontre hippique de chaque jour. En fait maintenant le monarque et sa famille quittent le Château de Windsor en voiture et ne montent dans les carrosses ouverts que dans la forêt de Windsor, peu avant le champ de courses.

Royal Ascot
Diese berühmte Rennstätte wird so genannt, weil sie auf königlichem Boden liegt. Seit 300 Jahren ist die königliche Familie bei den Rennen anwesend. Das Rennen findet seit Königin Anne, die einen Preis von 100 Guineen aussetzte, alljährlich im Juni statt. Den Rennen voraus geht eine vom Prinzgemahl eingeführte Prozession der Königsfamilie in Kutschen zum Renngelände.

THE WEDDING OF PRINCESS ANNE

On 14th November, 1973, Princess Anne and Captain Mark Phillips were married at Westminster Abbey, the then Archbishop of Canterbury, Dr Michael Ramsey, officiating at the ceremony. The Princess had driven with her father, the Duke of Edinburgh, from Buckingham Palace in the famous Glass Coach, with the Sovereign's Escort of Household Cavalry. Behind their coach came the Queen, with the Queen Mother and the Prince of Wales, in the Scottish State Coach, and behind them Princess Margaret and the Earl of Snowdon in the Irish State Coach. They were greeted at the Abbey door by the Dean of Westminster, to a fanfare composed by the Master of the Queen's Musick, Sir Arthur Bliss, performed by the band of the Queen's Dragoon Guards.

The newly married couple signed the register in Edward the Confessor's Chapel in the presence of the Queen and Queen Mother, the Prince of Wales and Prince Andrew, and the bridegroom's parents. Meanwhile, the massed choirs of Westminster Abbey and the Chapel Royal sang anthems composed by Handel and Vaughan Williams. Homage was then ceremonially paid to the Queen, in the Abbey, before the cortège returned along The Mall to Buckingham Palace.

Le mariage de la Princesse Anne
Le 14 novembre 1973 la Princesse Anne épousait le Capitaine Mark Phillips en l'Abbaye de Westminster. La Princess Anne était arrivée du Palais de Buckingham dans le fameux carrosse en verre, escortée par son père. Les nouveaux mariés signèrent ensuite le registre dans la Chapelle d'Edouard le Confesseur alors que les choeurs de l'Abbaye de Westminster et de la Chapelle Royale chantaient des hymnes de Handel et de Vaughan Williams.

Die Hochzeit von Prinzessin Anne
Am 14. November 1973 wurden Prinzessin Anne und Hauptmann Mark Phillips vom damaligen Erzbischof von Canterbury in einer grossartigen Zeremonie in der Westminster-Abtei getraut. Das junge Brautpaar trug sich in Gegenwart der führenden Mitglieder der Königsfamilie und der Eltern des Bräutigams in die Liste in der Kapelle Edwards des Bekenners ein.

THE ROYAL BIRTHDAY SALUTE, HYDE PARK

This military-royal occasion takes place in Hyde Park on several dates annually – on the anniversaries of the monarch's accession to the throne, of the coronation, and of the birthday. The King's Troop of the Royal Horse Artillery, under a Major acting as Commanding Officer for the day, goes into action. Six 13-pounder guns, each drawn by six horses, and dating from 1904, are hauled into position in pairs, under the immediate command of a Captain, Sergeant and three-man detachment; officers and men wear full dress uniform of fur busby, white plume, blue jacket frogged in gold, blue pantaloons with red stripe, spurred jackboots and white gloves. Other touches of colour include red collars and red 'bags' on the busbies.

The Royal Salute consists invariably of forty-one rounds fired precisely at intervals of ten seconds each from the preceding one, the first being fired at exactly eleven o'clock. The men in each detachment kneel on the grass, one leg thrust boldly forward, save for the man responsible for loading the 13-pounder. The wheeling of the guns into position, the removal of the horses and the actual firing are carried out with the precision for which this regiment has been famous down the years, controlled by an elaborate code of commands.

La salve pour l'anniversaire royal, Hyde Park
L'avènement au trône, le couronnement et l'anniversaire du monarque sont célébrés chaque année dans Hyde Park par une cérémonie royale et militaire. Le Salut Royal consiste invariablement de quarante et un coups de canon tirés à exactement dix secondes d'intervalle et le premier est tiré à onze heures précises. La Troupe du Roi du Royal Horse Artillery mène l'action avec toute la précision pour laquelle ce régiment est si célèbre.

Der königliche Geburtstagssalut im Hyde Park
Mehrmals im Jahr – an den Jahrestagen der Thronbesteigung, der Krönung und des Geburtstages der Königin – findet dieses Ereignis statt. Von der Königlichen Berittenen Artillerie werden sechs 13-Pfünderkanonen aus dem Jahre 1904 abgefeuert. Der königliche Salut besteht grundsätzlich aus 41 Runden, die im Abstand von je zehn Sekunden abgegeben werden. Der erste Schuss wird genau um 11 Uhr abgefeuert.

H.M. THE QUEEN AT COVENT GARDEN OPERA

This royal occasion portrays Her Majesty The Queen and the Duke of Edinburgh and other members of the Court, with a member of the Queen's personal bodyguard in attendance, entertaining the King and Queen of Belgium in May, 1963, in the Royal Box, gracing by their presence a capacity audience of well over 2,000 opera goers, almost all of them wearing evening dress.

First known as the Covent Garden Theatre, this splendid building stands in the heart of what was, until very recently, Covent Garden fruit and vegetable market and facing Bow Street Police Station – a fact which evokes comment especially from Italians accustomed to the setting of the famous Opera House at Milan. Opened in 1732, it was burnt down in 1808, rebuilt a year later as an opera house, burnt down again and again reopened in 1856. Since 1892 it has been called the Royal Opera House, the focal point of opera (and of ballet) in England. It occupies a site that was originally a spacious piazza surrounded by arcaded, Italian-style houses, some of which are still to be seen on the north side of the building. Near by is the 'actors' church, one of Inigo Jones's masterpieces, dedicated to St Paul.

Sa Majesté la Reine à l'Opéra de Covent Garden
Nous voyons ici la Reine et de Duc d'Edimbourg ainsi que d'autres membres de la famille royale recevant le Roi et la Reine de Belgique en mai 1963 dans la loge royale de Covent Garden. Toute l'assistance est bien sûr en tenue de soirée. Cet édifice splendide est au coeur de ce qui il n'y a pas si longtemps était les halles aux fruits et aux légumes. Anciennement le Covent Garden Theatre ouvert en 1732, il brûla en 1808; reconstruit il réouvrit un an plus tard comme opéra, brûla encore et fut à nouveau reconstruit et réouvert en 1856. Depuis 1892 il porte le nom de Royal Opera House.

Ihre Majestät an der Covent-Garden-Oper
Bei dieser Gelegenheit sehen wir die Königin, den Herzog von Edinburgh und andere Hofherrschaften zusammen mit dem belgischen Königspaar in der königlichen Loge. Das Covent Garden Theatre liegt im Herzen des ehemaligen Gemüsemarktes von Covent Garden und erinnert etwas an die berühmte Mailänder Oper. Es wurde 1732 eröffnet, brannte 1808 nieder, wurde neu errichtet und verbrannte erneut, ehe es 1856 wieder eröffnet wurde.

PRINCE CHARLES RECEIVING THE FREEDOM OF THE CITY OF LONDON

In the presence of the Lord Mayor and Sheriffs in their scarlet robes, the Prime Minister and other Ministers of State, diplomats, Lord Chief Justice and scores of other notabilities, H.R.H. The Prince of Wales received the Freedom of the City of London on 2nd March, 1971. Escorted by the Household Cavalry, he and Princess Anne had driven from Buckingham Palace to be officially welcomed by the Lord Mayor at Guildhall.

The Chamberlain, Richard Whittington (his name reminiscent of the 'Thrice-Lord-Mayor-of-London'), delivered the Address and presented to the newly elected Freeman 'This book containing the Rules for the Conduct of life prescribed for all Citizens of London', enclosed within a casket of gold ornamented with the *fleur de lys*, the emblem of the Prince of Wales. After the presentation, Prince Charles expressed his thanks to the Corporation for the honour conferred upon him, declaring that he was 'just one in a long line of suitably awed people who found it hard to express their gratitude upon such an occasion', adding that he would do his best to remain worthy of the honour all his life. After the ceremony, he and Princess Anne drove in an open carriage to the Mansion House for lunch with the Lord Mayor.

Le Prince de Galles est fait citoyen d'honneur de la Cité de Londres
Devant tous les hauts dignitaires de la Cité de Londres le Prince de Galles est fait citoyen d'honneur le 2 mars 1971. Le Chambellan prononce le discours et remet au Prince le livret contenant les règles de conduite prescrites à tous citoyens de Londres. Ce livret est renfermé dans un coffret en or à *Fleur de Lys*, emblème du Prince de Galles.

Der Prinz von Wales nimmt die Freiheit der Stadt London entgegen
Im Beisein des Oberbürgermeisters, der Kreisräte, des Ministerpräsidenten und anderer Minister, verschiedener Diplomaten, des Oberrichters und vielen anderen hohen Persönlichkeiten nahm der Prinz von Wales am 2. März 1971 die Freiheit der Stadt London entgegen. Er erhielt ein Buch mit Verhaltensregeln für alle Bürger Londons in einer goldenen Kassette mit der Wappenlilie, dem Abzeichen des Prinzen von Wales, und gelobte, sich dieser Ehre würdig zu erweisen.

THE STATE OPENING OF PARLIAMENT

One of the monarch's most important duties is the formal opening of each new parliamentary session, which is performed in the first week of November each year. It has always been, and remains, a ceremony carried out with stately ritual. Her Majesty, escorted by the Household Cavalry, makes the journey from Buckingham Palace in the Irish State Coach, and is welcomed by the Lord Great Chamberlain, the Lord Chancellor, and the Earl Marshal. Prior to her arrival, the vaults beneath the Houses of Parliament are ritually searched by the Yeomen of the Guard – a reminder of the Gunpowder Plot in 1605. Also, the Imperial State Crown, the Cap of State and the Sword of Maintenance have been delivered to the Royal Robing Room at the House of Lords.

The monarch, robed and crowned, enters the Upper House, thronged with Peers, Diplomats, Bishops, Judges and others, all wearing such robes and regalia as they are entitled to. The Loyal Commons are then summoned by Black Rod and file in, led by the Prime Minister of the day, the Leader of the Opposition, and the Speaker. The monarch then reads the Speech from the Throne, outlining the government's future policy. This is the most important example of the relationship between monarch and government to be publicly witnessed.

Ouverture officielle du Parlement

Une des premières tâches du monarque est l'ouverture officielle de chaque nouvelle session parlementaire qui se déroule la première semaine de novembre de chaque année. Cette cérémonie est toujours conduite selon un rite imposant. Après avoir été accueillie en grande cérémonie par le Grand Chambellan, le Grand Chancellier et le Grand Maréchal, la Reine en tenue d'apparat est escortée jusqu'au trône d'où elle lit le discours d'ouverture qui donne les grandes lignes de la prochaine politique gouvernementale.

Die staatliche Parlamentseröffnung

Eine der wichtigsten Pflichten der Königin ist die formelle Eröffnung einer neuen Parlamentsperiode in der ersten Novemberwoche jeden Jahres. Im Verlauf der Zeremonie verliest die Königin eine Rede, die die zukünftige Regierungspolitik umreisst. An diesem Beispiel verdeutlicht sich die Bindung zwischen Monarchie und Regierung.

THE QUEEN INSPECTS THE YEOMEN OF THE GUARD

This fine body of men constitutes the monarch's personal bodyguard. It was originally formed by Henry VII in 1485 from his 'faithful yeomen followers' who surrounded him at the Battle of Bosworth Field, and is thus the oldest military corps in existence. It has been responsible for the care of successive monarchs on their travels, serving in such intimate matters as tasting in advance the dishes set before them and guarding the royal bedchambers. The corps last accompanied the monarch on the battlefield at Dettingen, in 1743. They number 79 men, commanded by a Captain, Lieutenant and Adjutant drawn from the Army, Royal Marines and R.A.F.

The officers wear early nineteenth-century field officers' uniform, with an ebony stick personally presented by each monarch. The yeomen wear Tudor dress: scarlet tunic with gold-embroidered crown and royal cypher, knee-breeches, low-crowned velvet hat and ruff, and carry halberds. Among their duties is searching the vaults beneath the Houses of Parliament, since the Gunpowder Plot of 1605. They are also by tradition present at the Garter Ceremony at Windsor Castle and at the annual distribution of the Royal Maundy at Westminster Abbey.

La Reine passe en revue les hallebardiers de la garde du corps
Ce sont les gardes du corps personnels du monarque. Ce corps fut formé par Henri VII en 1485 et c'est à Dettingen qu'ils accompagnèrent pour la dernière fois le monarque sur le champ de bataille. Les officiers portent l'uniforme de combat des officiers du début du 19ème avec un bâton en bois d'ébène offert personnellement par chaque monarque. Les hommes revêtent l'uniforme Tudor et portent une hallebarde.

Die Königin inspiziert die königliche Leibwache
Diese Garde wurde 1485 von Henry VII ins Leben gerufen und ist somit das älteste noch bestehende Militärkorps. Die Leibwachter tragen Uniformen aus dem frühen 19. Jahrhundert. Neben der Teilnahme bei anderen Anlässen ist es seit Guy Fawkes' missglücktem Anschlag im Jahre 1605 ihre Aufgabe, vor der Parlamentseröffnung die Gewölbe des Parlamentsgebäudes zu durchsuchen.

THE CORONATION

Each successive monarch is 'consecrated Sovereign to his/her High Office' by the Archbishop of Canterbury, while seated on the Coronation Chair first used in 1308 by Edward II and containing the historic 'Stone of Scone'. There follows the Investiture with the Royal Robes and Insignia: the Sovereign's Sword, the Royal Sceptre, the Rod of Equity, the Orb and the Ring. Finally St Edward's Crown, the 'Emblem of Glory, Honour and Courage', is placed on the Sovereign's head by the Archbishop. The setting for this historic and moving ceremony is Westminster Abbey, an occasion of the utmost solemnity.

Following the consecration and crowning, the monarch moves to another seat, on a raised daïs, there to receive homage. Here H.M. The Queen still wears St Edward's Crown, though it will soon be replaced by the Imperial State Crown. On either side of her stand the then Bishop of Durham and Bishop of Bath and Wells, who since the accession of Richard I have preserved the hereditary right to 'support' thus the newly crowned monarch. The red robed figure kneeling before Her Majesty is Prince Philip, Duke of Edinburgh and Consort to the Queen, paying, as is his duty, homage to the monarch, as all must do, whether of high or low degree.

Le couronnement

C'est dans l'Abbaye de Westminster que chaque souverain consécutif est consacré par l'Archevêque de Canterbury. Le monarque est assis durant la cérémonie sur le Fauteuil du Couronnement inauguré en 1308 par le Roi Edouard II. Après la cérémonie d'investiture au cours de laquelle il reçoit l'Epée du Souverain, le Sceptre Royal, le Glaive de Justice, le Globe et l'Anneau et après les cérémonies de consécration et de couronnement, le souverain change de place pour recevoir les hommages de son peuple.

Die Krönung

Jeder neue Monarch wird zunächst, auf dem seit 1308 benutzten Krönungs-sessel sitzend, vom Erzbischof von Canterbury geweiht. Danach folgt die Investitur mit den königlichen Roben und den Zeichen der Königswürde. Dieser historische Anlass findet unter äusserster Feierlichkeit in der West-minster-Abtei statt. Die vor der Königin kniende Gestalt ist Prinz Philip, der wie alle anderen der Monarchin huldigen muss.

THE CHILDREN OF THE CHAPEL ROYAL

It was Henry VIII, himself a music lover and indeed a composer in his own right, who established a choir named the Children of the Chapel Royal, whose duties were to accompany him on his travels, though the choir is now permanently based in London. It numbers six 'Gentlemen in Ordinary' and ten 'Children of the Chapel', and their duties today consist of singing whenever required to do so on Royal Occasions that include religious services.

Appropriately enough in view of the period in which the choir was established, the boys wear Tudor costumes consisting of scarlet tunics trimmed with gold braid, scarlet knee-breeches, and black stockings and buckled shoes, though the men choristers wear scarlet cassocks and white surplices. The boys live in their London homes and when not on duty attend the City of London Day School, though officially they are attached to the Court. They are called upon to attend a number of Royal Occasions such as, for example, the christening of Prince Charles, the religious service on Armistice Day, and the wedding of Princess Anne and Captain Mark Phillips in Westminster Abbey. They also attend Her Majesty on the occasion of the Distribution of the Royal Maundy, whether in Westminster Abbey or at some other cathedral.

Les Enfants de la Chapelle Royale
C'est Henri VIII, lui-même grand amateur de musique et compositeur, qui a fondé ce choeur appelé les Enfants de la Chapelle Royale qui devait l'accompagner lors de ses voyages ; toutefois ce choeur est maintenant basé à Londres. Il compte six 'Gentlemen in Ordinary' et dix 'Children of the Chapel' et il est aujourd'hui chargé de chanter aux cérémonies royales qui comportent un service religieux.

Die Kinder der königlichen Kapelle
Dieser Chor wurde von Henry VIII, der Musik liebte und sogar Eigenkompositionen schrieb, ins Leben gerufen. Er besteht aus sechs Männern und zehn Knaben, deren Aufgabe es ist, bei königlichen Anlassen, wie z.B. der Taufe von Prinz Charles oder Prinzessin Annes Hochzeit zu singen.

THE BRAEMAR GATHERING

The Braemar Highland Society instituted this occasion a century and a half ago; it received Royal Approval when Queen Victoria graced it with her presence. It is held annually in the first week in September in Princess Royal Park, not far from the Royal Family's Highland Seat, Balmoral; there will always be at least one member of the Royals present, and usually more. Apart from Edinburgh itself, it offers the most splendid and spectacular occasion in Scotland.

Scottish music – that essentially of the bagpipers – dominates; the Highland pipe band shown in the picture is but one of the famous bands that will be called upon to perform. But the most exciting visual experience is of course the sequence of Highland Games. Among them are wrestling both in Cumberland and in catch-as-catch-can styles; throwing the hammer; putting the stone – all of these activities demanding immense brawn as well as skill. The most spectacular individual item is 'tossing the caber'. The caber is a Scots pine log some twenty feet in length and weighing anything up to two hundredweight. The record 'toss' is that of a caber weighing no less than 230 pounds; such a feat called for not only outstanding strength but an astonishing sense of balance and accurate timing into the bargain.

La réunion Braemar
Cette réunion a lieu annuellement au cours de la première semaine de septembre et elle se tient dans Princess Royal Park, pas très loin du château royal de Balmoral en Ecosse. C'est un des évènements écossais des plus splendides et des plus spectaculaires. Outre la musique écossaise et tout particulièrement les joueurs de cornemuse qui y dominent, on peut y voir aussi les Jeux des Highlands: la lutte et le lancement du marteau. Toutefois c'est le 'tossing the caber', le lancement d'un tronc de pin, qui demeure le plus spectaculaire et le plus pittoresque.

Das Treffen von Braemar
Dieses Treffen, das alljährlich im September im schottischen Hochland stattfindet, ist eines der glänzendsten Schauspiele ausserhalb Edinburghs. Neben Dudelsackmusik gibt es die sogenannten Highland Games mit einer Vielzahl von Wettbewerben wie Ringen, Hammerwerfen und dem besonderen Spektakel des Baumstammwerfens. Der schwerste je hochgestämmte und geworfene Baumstamm wog volle 230 Pfund.

PRESENTATION OF NEW COLOURS TO THE SCOTS GUARDS

Since regimental Colours are frequently paraded and often travel widely, it becomes necessary at intervals ranging from ten to fifteen years to replace the Old Colours by New Colours. The presentation is deemed important enough to be carried out usually by the reigning monarch or at least some member of the Royal Family. In this picture, H.M. The Queen is presenting New Colours to the 2nd Battalion, Scots Guards, appropriately enough in the grounds of her Palace of Holyroodhouse, Edinburgh, on 30th June, 1965.

Like all such ceremonies, this presentation is carried out with dignity and a strict regard for military procedure and ritual. First, the Old Colours are 'marched off parade'. The New Colours are then 'marched on to parade', uncased from their protective sheath and draped over the drum laid side-downwards on the turf, there to be consecrated by the Chaplain to the battalion, with other clergy present. The New Colours are then formally presented to the monarch, who in turn presents them to an officer in full regimentals, kneeling and flanked by two brother officers. The New Colours are then ceremonially 'marched past', at first in slow time, then in quick time.

Présentation des nouvelles couleurs aux gardes écossais
Sa Majesté la Reine présente les Nouvelles Couleurs au 2ème Bataillon des Gardes Ecossais au Palais de Holyroodhouse à Edimbourg. En effet les couleurs s'usant assez rapidement il faut les remplacer à intervalle de 10 à 15 ans. On fait tout d'abord défiler les Vieilles Couleurs, puis on présente ensuite les Nouvelles Couleurs au monarque qui à son tour les présente à un officier en grand uniforme agenouillé devant lui et flanqué de deux autres officiers.

Vergabe von neuen Uniformen an die Scots Guards
Aus der Notwendigkeit, die alten Uniformen alle zehn bis fünfzehn Jahre gegen neue zu wechseln, wurde ein feierlicher Anlass mit grosser Würde und strengem Ritual. Das Bild zeigt die Ubergabe neuer Uniformen an das 2. Bataillon der Scots Guards durch Königin Elizabeth am 30. Juni 1965 in Edinburgh.

TROOPING THE COLOUR

H.M. The Queen is Colonel-in-Chief of the Life Guards, Royal Horse Guards, Grenadier Guards, Coldstream Guards and the Scots, Welsh and Irish Guards. Annually on her 'official birthday', the second Saturday in June, she rides in state from Buckingham Palace, attended by the Sovereign's Mounted Escort, to Horse Guards Parade in Whitehall. The Household Cavalry and the Brigade of Guards await her. On arrival, she mounts a white horse and, escorted by mounted officers in full regimentals, proceeds to inspect the Guards and take their salute to a background of music from massed bands. She herself wears the uniform of the particular regiment whose Colours are being 'trooped' – this being done annually in strict rotation. Having taken the salute, she dismounts and returns in state to the palace with her escort.

The ceremony was instituted by George II and designed to be a loyal salute to the occupant of the throne, in public. The Colours trooped are those that each regiment fought under on the field of battle, serving as a rallying-point either for attack or last-ditch stand. To this day, the reigning monarch is closely associated with them in an official capacity.

Parade du drapeau

Montée sur un cheval blanc, sa Majesté la Reine, Colonel-en-Chef de plusieurs régiments de Gardes, passe les troupes en revue le jour de son anniversaire officiel le deuxième samedi de juin. Elle porte elle-même l'uniforme du régiment dont les couleurs sont présentées. Le drapeau de chaque régiment est présenté à tour de rôle d'année en année.

Die Fahnenparade

Die Königin bekleidet den Rang eines kommandierenden Oberst der verschiedenen königlichen Garden. Jedes Jahr an ihrem offiziellen Geburtstag reitet sie zur Fahnenparade zum Horse Guards Parade, wo jeweils ein Regiment durch die Abnahme seiner bestimmten Fahne geehrt wird.

CHANGING THE GUARD AT BUCKINGHAM PALACE

When the monarch is in residence, the Royal Standard flies above the palace. One or other of the Guards regiments will be taking its turn of duty according to the strict rota. At eleven o'clock each morning the New Guard, in dress uniform and preceded by the Guards' Band, advances towards the Old Guard to the music of its regimental slow march. An officer carries the Regimental Colour. As might be expected, the ceremony of the change-over is executed with a ritual formality that is marked by extreme precision, as well as being very colourful.

There is a formal reciprocation of what may be termed 'military courtesies'; presenting of arms between the Old and the New Guard is accompanied by clicking of heels and, in the background, by appropriate martial music. The new sentries are posted, while the officers responsible for the exchange of duties march rigidly up and down the Fore Court in pairs. The sentries who have just been relieved – the Old Guard – rejoin their fellows and march towards the main gateway, still to the accompaniment of the regimental slow march music. Immediately they pass through the gateway, this changes to the regimental quick march.

Changement de la garde au Palais de Buckingham
Cette cérémonie a lieu chaque matin à onze heures quand le monarque est au Palais (dans ce cas le drapeau est hissé). La nouvelle Garde, en uniforme d'apparat et précédée de la musique de la Garde, vient relever l'ancienne Garde.

Wachablösung am Buckingham-Palast
Wenn die Königin anwesend ist, weht die königliche Standarte über dem Palast, und nach einem strengen Dienstplan übernimmt eines der Garderegimenter die Wache. Jeden Morgen um elf Uhr findet die Wachablösung mit ritueller Formalität und allen militärischen Ehrenbezeigungen statt. Zu den Klängen des jeweiligen Regimentsmarsches tritt die neue Wache an und die alte zieht ab.

THE BLUES AND ROYALS DISMOUNTING THE QUEEN'S LIFE GUARD

The detachment approaching the camera down The Mall from Buckingham Palace is known as the Short Guard; the unit mounts guard when (as may be seen from the absence of the Royal Standard at the mast head) the Queen is not in residence. 'The Blues' and 'The Royals' consist of the amalgamation of the Royal Horse Guards and the 1st Dragoons. The first-named derive their name from the fact that, uniquely in the early regular army, when red prevailed, their uniform was blue; they were the favourite regiment of King George III. The Royal Horse Guards were created the official Household Cavalry in 1821, in recognition of their valour at Waterloo in 1815.

The Royals were designated by Charles II 'Our Owne Royall Regiment' in 1683 and granted precedence in battle over all other Line Cavalry. It was they who captured a French regiment's Eagle Standard; to this day this feat is commemorated by their wearing of the Royal Eagle on the left sleeve of their dress uniform. They wear red-plumed helmets and – a nice touch – the officers' chargers have a black 'beard' attached to the jowl-piece, a reminder of the 'beard' worn by Royal Dragoon chargers when this was still a Mounted Cavalry Regiment.

Ce détachement que l'on voit approcher monte la garde quand le monarque n'est pas au Palais. 'The Blues' et 'The Royals' sont un mélange de Royal Horse Guards et des 1ers Dragoons. Régiment favori du Roi Georges III, les premiers reçurent le nom de 'Blues' du fait de la couleur de leur uniforme. En 1683 Charles II désignait les Royals comme 'Notre propre régiment royal' et leurs accorda dans les batailles la précédence sur tout autre régiment de cavalerie.

Die königliche Gardekavallerie und das 1. Dragonerregiment geben die königliche Wache ab
Diese beiden Regimenter erwiesen sich als besonders tapfer in Schlachten, wie z.B. 1815 bei Waterloo, und wurden deshalb von den verschiedenen Monarchen mit besonderer Hochachtung behandelt und entsprechend geehrt.

A STATE VISIT

The Queen is here seen riding in one of the State Landaus with General Yakabu Gowon, in June, 1973, on the occasion of his State Visit to this country.

Heads of State are customarily welcomed on arrival by Her Majesty or the Duke of Edinburgh. In this instance the Queen and the General drove in an open landau from Victoria Station by way of Parliament Square, Whitehall and the Admiralty Arch and thence along The Mall to Buckingham Palace. It is interesting to note that until the opening of Trafalgar Square, only as long ago as 1841, The Mall was sealed off at each end, the only official access to Buckingham Palace being by way of Horse Guards; this is why, to this day, the reigning monarch's Life Guard (originally the Troop of Horse Guards) is still mounted there.

Une visite officielle de chef d'Etat
La Reine est ici en compagnie du Général Yakabu Gowon lors de sa visite officielle en juin 1973. Sa Majesté La Reine et le Duc d'Edimbourg accueillent en général les chefs d'état en visite officielle. Il est intéressant de noter que jusqu'en 1841 le Mall était fermé aux deux extrémités et que la seule voie d'accès officiel au Palais de Buckingham passait par les Horse Guards. C'est pour cette raison qu' aujourd'hui encore la garde est montée ici.

Ein Staatsbesuch
Hier sehen wir die Königin zusammen mit dem nigerianischen Staatschef General Yakubu Gowon in einer Staatskutsche anlässlich seines England-besuches im Juni 1973. Staatsoberhäupter werden traditionesgemäss bei ihrer Ankunft entweder von der Königin oder dem Herzog von Edinburgh begrüsst.

PRINCE PHILIP BEING PIPED ABOARD A NAVAL VESSEL

Prince Philip has a long naval tradition behind him. During World War Two he served both in Home Waters and the Mediterranean, the Far East and the Pacific; he is an Admiral of the Fleet and takes every possible opportunity of visiting naval vessels, at home and abroad.

The ritual of Piping Aboard (strictly 'Piping the Side') dates back to 1645. A naval officer paying a courtesy visit from his own ship would be hoisted from the launch in a 'bosun's chair'; as it drew level with the deck, the bosun would 'give orders' on his pipe to the crew handling the operation. The pipe consists of a curved silver tube known as the 'buoy', mounted on an ornamental plate known as the 'keel'. It is possible to produce from this a succession of trills, known as 'chirps', on an ascending and then descending scale, notes drawn-out or brief, with varying pitch. The pipe is still used for the welcoming on board of any distinguished visitor. But in former times it was used to issue orders in recognisable code form to both seamen and fighting-men aboard ship; the note was so high-pitched and distinctive that it could be heard above the roar of guns and the rattle of musketry.

Le Prince Philip a derrière lui une longue tradition navale et il saisit toute occasion de visiter un vaisseau de la marine. La tradition du 'Piping Aboard' (jouer de la flûte pour accueillir quelqu'un qui monte à bord) remonte à 1645. Dans la marine britannique on joue toujours de la flûte pour accueillir un visiteur de marque, mais autrefois on l'utilisait pour donner des ordres en code.

Prinz Philip wird mit der Pfeife an Bord eines Marineschiffes begrüsst
Prinz Philip kann auf eine lange Karriere bei der Marine zurückblicken. Er hat den Rang eines Flottenadmirals und nutzt jede Gelegenheit Marineschiffe zu besuchen. Früher wurden mit der Pfeife Befehle in Form eines Codes erteilt; heute wird sie dazu benutzt, hohe Besucher an Bord zu begrüssen.

PRINCESS ANNE PRESENTING LEEKS TO WELSH GUARDS

The last of the Guards Brigades to be formed was the Welsh. Its nucleus was drawn from one hundred Welshmen serving in the four other brigades. On 26th February 1915, King George V duly named it, and it first mounted guard at Buckingham Palace three days later, appropriately enough on 1st March, St David's Day. Their first Colours were presented to them on 3rd August 1915; a fortnight later they carried them into battle on the Western Front. The Welsh Guards fought on the Somme, at Ypres, Arras and Loos; and in World War II they covered the flank of the army during the evacuation from Dunkirk.

The wearing of the leek is a part of their tradition. Annually on the Sunday nearest to St David's Day a leek is presented to every member of the brigade, almost invariably by a member of the Royal Family. In this picture, Princess Anne is handing a box of leeks to a senior officer in full dress uniform. A notable feature of the Welsh Guards uniform is the green-and-white plume worn on the bearskin. Another feature that perhaps only the keen-eyed observer will detect is the fact that the tunic buttons are not spaced equidistantly but in two groups of five, as may actually be seen on the three main officers' tunics here.

La Princesse Anne offre des poireaux aux Gardes Gallois
La Brigade des Welsh Guards a été formée en 1915 et c'est le Roi Georges V qui lui a donné son nom. Elle a servi dans les deux guerres mondiales. L'emblême du poireau a un rapport direct avec cette Brigade et on en présente un à chacun de ses membres le dimanche le plus proche du jour de la Saint David (le 1er mars). Ici nous voyons la Princesse Anne en train de présenter les poireaux.

Prinzessin Anne überreicht den Welsh Guards Lauchstengel
Die Brigade der Welsh Guards wurde 1915 gegründet und von König George V benannt. Der Lauchstengel ist traditionell mit dieser Brigade verbunden, und jedes Mitglied erhält einen an dem St. Davids-Tag (1. März) nächsten Sonntag. Hier überreicht Prinzessin Anne die Lauchstengel.